ARROWS
Go Thru
HEARTS

Selected Poems
1970-1995

WILL STAPLE

Six Ft. Swells Press

After Hours Poetry

Arrows Go Through Hearts
Copyright 2017 © Will Staple
First Edition

Six Ft. Swells Press
www.AfterHoursPoetry.com
www.facebook.com/SixFtSwells

Book & Cover Design: Julie Valin, The Word Boutique,
www.TheWordBoutique.net

ISBN-13: 978-0985307554
ISBN-10: 0985307552

Dedicated to John Montoya, a Havasaupai, and Jeff Whitt,
who typed up every single poem for free

to Rebekah & Radu

Will Staple

Note From the Author

These poems were selected from about 200 works published between 1970 and 1995. They were wildly popular when read aloud to a wide variety of Northern California audiences. I look back on the anarcho-taoist simplicity with awe, an artifact of a culture intact, a majestic ruin of moments that refuse to die.

There is something to be learned in sweat lodges that can't be put into words. There is a tenderness that children teach us that makes all organized religions shameful. There is a truth beyond the blood-soaked, civilized abstractions that manipulative spin doctors disregard. There is a truth all governments fear that even a single uneducated mother might realize, and so they need armies and prisons and lies to continue to exist.

The attention listeners give to songs or poems invents a tribe for as long as the songs are in the air, an experience accessible to any teenager listening to a popular melody, feeling juicy to be alive. With the delicate edge of a recognizing grin, it is juicy to be alive, so I hold a torch against the wind. Let me take you right straight thru.

≈

Contents

Foreword   i
Introduction   iii

I.

Delicate Edge

Coming Out of the Woodrose Cafe 1
Shen Tao 2
Raven 3
passes for human 4
Dream 5
Sierra Buttes '87 6
Little Cloud 7
dried bird claw 8
wind 9
may seem dull 10
Neither the speaker nor the spoken 11
Mexican Warning 12
Crying in Your Pillow, or Only One More Heartbreak Left 13
practical solution 15
outclassed 16
Eastern Mysticism 17
the solution 18
a bruised peach 19
Work Song 20
Joanne 21

II.

A Torch Against the Wind

Why should the gods demand? .25
Poetry 26
Take a poet home 27
Either Mountain Lion or Chickens? 28
trail not maintained, use at own risk 29
tobacoba trail 30
From the Song "Come Across" .31
Formerly a Deer 32
Mudra 33
Alone in Camp 34
Do You Live for Yourself, or for Others? 35
Rattlesnake Woman 36

The Fearful, Accurate Vision of a Hunted, Marked Man 37
You Get Irritated 38
Savor Further In 39
I call my spirits and they all come quick 40
500 Dakini 41
Dead Cat Head 42
First Supai Poem 43
Indian Granary Circle 44
Old Ways 45
"The Delighted Dancer Filled With Rapture" 46
Fertility level 47
Melon 48
Wild Song 49
Petroglyphs 50
before words, understanding 51
Wisdom Road 52
So-called Spirit Helpers 53
Coyote 54
Nov 17 Sutra 55
I went to see the sage 57
Omen Bearer 58
The Deer 59
El Venado 60
Red Rock Road 61
Excerpts from Bristlecone Pine .62
Dissolute But Not Extinct 64
Poem of a CPITS Poet Working 65
Second Part of Dr. Montoya's Sermon 66
Already Wet 67
Stuck craw 68
Rooster Song 69
Died on the Trail 70
Montoya Powwow 71
To Fall To 72

III.

Right Straight Through

Recognizing Looks 75
Invite 76
"Remember the Poor - It Costs Nothing" 77
Skunky 78
Him 79
Right Straight Thru 80

The More I Stare 81
3 Sisters 82
Waits 83
The Woman of Dawu 84
Some Other 86
Someone else's touch 87
There Are Tests 88
Venus in Scorpio 89
By the time 90
Afraid of Showing 91
I Hate the Men You Sleep With 92
Small Doses 93
Thank You 94
If 95
When Coyote 96
Supervisor 97
16 Days 98
"Dear Ben" 99
Sierra Love Note 100

IV.

Recognizing Grin

How the Mattole River Rd. Got Open 103
None of my consideration 104
John Montoya's Final Benediction 105
Ode to a Medicine Man, George Staple, died 11/4/89 108
No More Hot Coffee When I Die 109
Ancient Mastery 110
Why Crime is Unavoidable 111
Self-Fulfilling Prophecy 112
Law-Abiding 113
The Only Way To Reduce Crime is to Make Fewer Acts Illegal 114
Hard Being So Good 115
Thief 116
Four Stones 117
Come Now 118
Zendo Meadow 119
Polar Bear Head #1 120
Poem Requested by Nanao to be Put on a Scarf 121
North from Shelter Cove 122

Acknowledments   125
About the Author   127

Foreword

I have followed Will Staple's unique, cranky, original poetry since we first met in the Sixties. He has carved out a special niche for himself, with his poems of love, pain, pyschological exploration, Buddhist practice, rattlesnake wisdom and coyote integrity.

Will's book, *Arrows Go Thru Hearts*, has his particular original signature: something is here that belongs to the world of shamanism, deep power, a certain kind of sexual energy, a certain kind of rebellion. Many of the poems in this collection are subtle with pain, but a pain mastered if not transmuted; wry admission of his own culpability woven into it. Will Staple's steadiness and commitment to poetry is peerless. Even deeper, even more impressive, is his commitment to the craft that lies beyond, behind, and within art. He gambles for the harder truths, and brings them back to the daylight world. "Doctors recognize doctors."

–Gary Snyder

Introduction

An Artist's Evolution

As a publisher, there is a certain joy to bringing a twenty-five year poetic adventure to the page for all to delight in. It is an opportunity open to the world to admire a revered poet from his earliest writings and inclinations, and to observe a true artist through his exploits, discoveries and every day normalities.

In this collection of poems, Will's exercises and experiments in spirituality, poetry, wilderness, love and living allow us to see the poet as he truly is—a craftsman. Building worlds in words over an extended period of time. Constructing and reconfiguring experiences, emotions and images into a foundational work on which they can stand. We are offered a peek at the evolution of an artist: raw, adventurous, broken, beaming, sincere and shape-shifting. Readers of this collection will hear the changing of one poet's voice and state of mind, see the altering of style and substance of poetry lived from cabins to canyons, mountains, meadows, zendos and forests, through interactions with friends and lovers who remain, and those that have long departed. There is a simplicity and wildness in these poems that keeps them vibrant and alive.

The highest compliment I can give Will Staple is to assure him that "I'll quote him somewhere further up the trail." This is how great poetry lives on.

–Todd Cirillo, Co-Publisher, Poet
6/2/17 11:48pm

I.

Delicate Edge

Coming Out of the Woodrose Cafe

for Andy Steele

The smiling buddha came riding into town
    in the back of a pickup truck
        in the rain,

the smile cut into the face
      as deep as the falling cut
        in a tree,

bare breasts perky over the slope
  of a belly
conversant with all the pleasures of life
    and full
        with whatever the world offers.

Shen Tao

Shen Tao was not afraid because he didn't care
he didn't try to please
     yet got around to doing his share
he wasn't proud enough to be discontented
  but took what came with pleasure, and
     soon forgot what wasn't there.

≈

Raven

I knew her down near Sonoma State,
smell of fields and trees, in a fixed-up chicken coop
so the windows were a little low.
Shy to her assured poise
it got hard to breathe near her quiet eyes
or at least breathe harder.
The windows were open to cool off,
we were sitting on her bed,
she had long black hair, black expectant eyes.
she was talking quietly
and her voice had a soft musical quality.
She was calmly telling me truths about myself
nothing a hand or face or star date would tell her
but with real concern
getting right down to where my blood pounded
my heart to feel my life as I do
calling my shots and telling me who I was.

She looked at me then in a way irresistible
a promise of everything satisfying
religious and erotic.
I looked at her in a trance of lust
my eyes sort of crossed and my mouth crooked
she blew in my face
and puffed out her chest
somewhere I saw feathers
and remembered something like this:
"We'll do it your way, I want to do it
like you deep down want to do it."
"You're an enchanted creature?" I asked
for the first time suspecting I was in a dream.
"Yes, coyote," her head made a birdlike gesture
ducking under her hair like a shoulder of wing.
"I'm Raven,"
she smiled confidently,
"and I'm going to make you rave."

❧

passes for human

yes, i am an old coyote
not yet well into my useless years.
o, i fool them, wearing clothes
standing upright, talking like a man.

i look over behind me and move pretty fast
        for an old timer
            no longer a coy pup.

not that i've changed my ways
the mind is on fire
red eyed, burning.
i even feel more like being me.

whatever i had got me this far
this is what's left of what there was...
        a survivor.

Dream

('69, Riverside)

First time i saw the "old man" so clearly.
Here, in this room, didn't seem at first like
    a dream, that i had awoke.
in ancient filthy rags
sitting in the corner on the floor
where your cone basket is.
when he got up
      bugs and ants scattered.
He was past expression
      of all the petty feelings
with the self assurance of a dog
      who doesn't mind starving.
Silent, dispassionate, absently—
i saw him wander your front yard.

                             ~

Sierra Buttes '87

Preaching simplicity
"All you need is the flesh on your bones
and an attention to the day's unfolding
revelation"

Pine needles shimmer in the tops of trees
sunbeams pierce the branches
We breathe deep, climbing steepens

"A forgiving gratitude
with a quivering
delicate edge"
is what I call it.

Lowell also claims, "Exertion is pleasure"
I assure him I'll quote him
somewhere further up the trail.

꠹

Little Cloud

grand canyon '71

little cloud, that appears from nowhere
little   Cloud   called passion
disappears   for no reason.
   intangible substance   that again returns,
over and turns   back to nothing
   disappears to   reappear
what is the meaning   of the smell of
loosened hair and skin sunned now lying
   in the shade with she who strokes
and laughs at a   sly smile little cloud,
again it goes just as i sense the meaning, just
 as i see it as it is.

dried bird claw

dried bird claw
found within a dead snake's desert dried skin
in a chimney between two cliffs in a sheer
tower's side, only way up.   dried bird claw
found on finding the way
                              down, after looking
over edges from slanting out downward ledges,
claw which relieved my fear of dying
stranded and waterless, the spirits waiting
until full power of night to attack, swarming
the thirsty mind with fear.
dried bird claw   the way back
the feel of fearing to fall, where you live
by care   aware that life
        can suddenly end
dizzy of height and balancing in the wind
trusting   rock and body to hold
        another instant.

wind

a path
like the current in the sea
like a stream
wind says:

   "I want to show you
what has been
    but i want you to see
    unrelated to yourself
see without thinking
    listen   without
getting ready to speak."

may seem dull

When we go on runs we come back
   with what we need
wood fence materials, food
   it may seem dull to you
wood stoves   mason jars
   bare walnut trees in sunset.

gas, beer, what is money for?
   traveling over old Stage lines
   doctoring ancient sweat lodge sites
a lost race, returning
   raise from the dead
         sung back to life
like ancestors descendants
   evoking
            what we came for

those who go out for strong medicine
      get it
or do not come back at all.

Neither the speaker nor the spoken
the seer nor the seen
nor any discrimination whatsoever

the hopalong cassidy pocket watch hangs at the right time
the old glass in the east, the only window
casts wavering light on the bare board floor
the door bangs
the 5 gallons of leaking water are on the porch
the fly is ignored because it is not a mosquito
the water in the quart jar is good
the smoke rolling is put off
every possession cries to be hung up
the walls crack
the candle burns, the sun rises
the shade lasts
the ant is only a scout and will not find
a dirty bowl.

Mexican Warning

when you gain temporary control
of this universe
mere mortal
who possesses powerful eyes
do not inflict illness unintentionally
just by looking at someone
admiringly or with envy.

when it comes to you, that power
  can change into a jaguar
    counsel kings
  stop catastrophes
cleanse the bewitched.

be courteous
inconspicuous
don't permit yourself excessive wealth.

Crying in Your Pillow,
or Only One More Heartbreak Left

She saw me on the trail as the young
    indians on horseback recognized me
        sitting in the shade before the switchbacks.

She had a dobie bitch on a leash
    and was staring at me
        when I looked up. Our eyes held.

Before I knew it she was sitting down
    talking to me, the coyote
        thirty years on this same trail out.

Everything I do is always watched
    no wonder I search the distant places
        where water is measured in cups.

She left with her address in my hand
    I knew not how. Even coyote
        is vulnerable to entrancement
        susceptible to her spell.

Watching me all the time
    not only my enemies, my friends
        quickly are concerned.

Coming up out   into the open
    two of my oldest most trusted
        men I have know for decades:

"You better not like her, coyote,"
    they can always read my mind.
"She's not for you."
    "Her body was whispering,"
        I said
        picking up the scent
        playing the part.

"You need a woman
    older and uglier, coyote—
the young ones mostly leave
    you crying in your pillow.

"We're your friends,
your heart's been broken too much—
    you got
only one more heartbreak left."

practical solution

it is easy to love perfection
but if you can find in your mate

her most graceless imperfection, her ugliness
    and cherish that...

    you have deluded yourself

but can endure
the most intolerable of situations.

ॐ

outclassed

"i may not have anything special
but you don't got nothin' special yourself"

if either of us did
we would certainly have the taste

    to conceal it perfectly
so as not to make the other
    uncomfortable.

Eastern Mysticism

what good did getting up
every morning at 5:30 to
    meditate   do?
      your girlfriend
        left you.

the solution

if the mouse
gnawing on nuts under your bed
annoys,
listen harder.

a bruised peach

i threw away a bruised peach
   in reaction to a disordered camp.
now i regret, in my solitary waterless shack
   dusty and fly infested, having done so.

when asked what i was going to do with my lover
   who had left me for one who likewise left her
i should have confessed that i had eaten bruised peaches
   and as i came out of the desert without food
if i found a dried date that other men had handled,
   cast off and let fall to the ground
that i would not hesitate in the least
   to brush it off and stick it in my mouth
for my faith assures me it will be just as sweet.

Work Song

the eyes on the nail
pull the hammer in the hand.
the sand makes cement bond
because it remembers how it was
to be an uncrushed stone.

Joanne

when i couldn't call
in the snow storm
you prayed "let him be safe
even in someone else's arms"

you told me to see my old lover
because you trusted my heart.
we're no longer afraid.

we've even got over hiding
our wimpy side
somehow even more endearing
than the polished, considerate
sultry, witty one
we display in public.

how comfortable
to wake with someone
you really know.

II.

A Torch Against the Wind

Why should the gods demand?

there is a way the gods
        want us to sit
stewing in our own juices
an iron pot set solidly on the fire.

not in retaliation or reaction
the neck down the back not tense-
anxiety breathed---expelled in the next breath.
    they wait deliberately
    with patience we do not have---
        to calmly speak---when we slow
enough   to hear.

why should one who is beyond
  the reach of praise
        waste words
    on a distracted listener?
why should the gods demand
we assume an attentive attitude
unless they be ready
    to spill the goods?

Poetry

I no longer write poems
but let them drag me out
   spell me to their use.
Not that i live for anything else
but poetry no longer holds hidden rewards
no angelic millionairess will discover me
   to banish need from my life
no exclusive fellowship
with those who think they're something
      will enchant me.
It's true, poets are exposed to flattery
    which i shamelessly enjoy
but no one understands my obscurest poems
which all agree are my worst
which i like best.
my poems and i do incest
    bask in our lust
   seduce me in my craving
i hope this seduction can be shared
   tho the poems themselves don't care.

Take a poet home

take a poet home with you tonight
he has traveled 3,000 miles to be here
even further---out of the vast
distance of shy despair---
thru the tongue-tied preparation
    for ridicule, apprehension

the poet has emerged momentarily
from the dungeon of his repression.
   he hovers temporarily above
what pulls him down
      back into---
   floats, his head
     no weight for the spine
   heart open
       longing
light...

if you want to, whisper what you feel
in the poet's ear
    while he is here
so that he may not forget you

      ever.

Either Mountain Lion or Chickens?

you should feel honored
   that a mountain lion
   (who travels 200 miles in a week)
    could find such as you
the least bit worthy
to honor with her presence

old doctors had such protectors
bear rattlesnake lion, they knew
eagle hawk personally even   coyote

because a wild beast can howl
in the midst of civilization
human beings, facing extinction,
may survive their own cleverness.

if you kill what is more than human
how much is your life worth?

trail not maintained, use at own risk

land that makes you tough, shares its beauty
                    solitude, when you take it, takes you
quietly into beauty
lending deeper perspectives by example
        endless in its enduring grace.

this calm we leave only to return to
    taking as much quiet with us as we can.
    future social demands
        trouble people give
            or you give yourself by not giving
like the distant waterless stretch near nightfall,
    can be run down and passed over
            while just enough light
water and final burst of strength remain
to come back with what you went for
            as well as making it back.

we take when we feel need,   take when we feel a lack,
take when others take so as not to be taken,
but when you have enough   you can give
                    from the heart
            what you hide
        when you hold back love.

tobacoba trail

i don't drink all the time
but when i do
i like a sixpack or two
talking straight on
no threatening interruptions darkening
        a calmed nondualistic mind
and no one to get in my way.

From the Song "Come Across"

come across or i go over. i gotta sing cause i hear voices
in the rapids of the waterfall below here, falling
as it does under several logs spanning the river
or stuck out in space.   four legger hear me;

i know you can understand my words, you were
men we sing to, who help us in our dreams.
come across—pine tree tops reflected in the water-
or i go over.   to your way of thinking.   hunter;

don't shoot me, i don't want to die, i'm a human
because i can sing but i look like an animal to you,
that's why i'm telling you not to shoot,
animals in the bodies of humans. no humans left.

i was a trail traveler, the trail
has long since ceased to exist.

Formerly a Deer

man ceases to be a deer
with indoor heating
so drinks.

Mudra

She who turns you on   in the
right direction, lights you up, makes you
interested, interesting
   any moment of concentration
potency, poignancy, poise.

   up a steep thicket of
manzanita, poison oak,   oak
all grown together   sweating
   the deer can get thru   so
so can you, always   fair
   even if she's hard, climbing
a rock face   can be done
even if there's only one way
step by step, just.

She who brought you thru
ecstasy seven times one morning
and who was never seen again.

Alone in Camp

to at last be left
with intense, reflection   on breath
just me, knotted, tense or free
          for a moment.   quite attentive
      to how short life is
              how easy to waste it.
i sit in a small hut on a hill
            side of a canyon
              miles from a paved road
                  waiting for the moon to come
      after the first fall rain.

If a friend paid a debt
    i could buy bottlecaps, malt
        fill up my car with gas.
      but it's too much to go to town,
now   it's getting cool enough to write,
the dry season's over, letters due.

it's better if you go   to give.
some feel threatened in their own space
if you go to take.

best to wait and graciously receive—
patience is the quickest way
            but beings need looking after.

Do You Live for Yourself, or for Others?

nobody matters, drink all you want,
you're alone when you face death
no one loves you enough to save
    your life, if they could
      you would leave.
o creature who lives outdoors
    on food he finds, never stealing
      as is the human custom
when you look into an aimed arrow's
    shaft, at a hand made point
      or the 32 special indian rifle
        IS it better to die?
        o no, come along

you cannot leave   it   hangs on
your face, in your throat, how
    you posture, feel about other people,

    all   you think you are
you know at least that is untrue
    tell me how i seem
      it will be uncomfortable
      and i will feel
    as if i'm learning
      something.

Rattlesnake Woman

rattlesnake woman
please don't strike me with your venom.

my medicine that cured
you found an antidote for.
you cast a spell it could not heal.

o rattlesnakes
waiting in the shade of the hot sun
don't cut me down.

from sadness inside i know i taste bad
i'm no competition for tastier prey.
            consider me not
as i pass thru your land.

The Fearful, Accurate Vision of a
Hunted, Marked Man

"entirely for their own sakes
tell others when they lie,
violently use their spirit to
dismember and belittle you."

"but do not contend
victory's more terrible than defeat

if tricked into annihilating
by strength, the foe
thus vanquished
would then be vindicated?"

"give them no power
see thru them as if
they had already gone below."

You Get Irritated

when words pass by from the inaccessible one,

a dismayed look, not happy to see anyone, miserable
he stares into faces with a look of disbelief or suspicion;
brooding and alert, yet still
              straining to become more aware
as if that would ease the strain.

       aid the afflicted, ease a burden. calm distress.

demons of all forms float through his mind. his truth
is a two edge sword that wounds him to use
even if he were   fearless of retaliation.

          yet these same weaknesses,
       when the dark spell breaks,
       make the gleam of rays glowing from
       his smiling eyes   enough to heal.

Savor Further In

trance tune
goes out the door
        across the yard
bounces off the tree
falls back down here
  from where in trance we sing
a gentleman
enjoying well his delight
        savor
further in   than inside
filling up the
heft
of the body
swaying with the
        spine bones
            a little further apart.

I call my spirits and they all come quick

I call my spirits
they come quick

breathe on me!
blow me all out--
heal, make whole!

Spirits
come quick.

500 Dakini

500 dakini
waiting in the world
　　when called
500 dakini
came forth

long before the international bodhisattva movement
was worship to Saraswati;
wind thru woods, falling water-
living sounds in air
　-mold and shape
seen in the form of a called young girl:
　　　creative woman
　　　　　　clear eyes
　　　aware smile, attentive calm
　　　　　watchful
　　　as if looking out for her young.

"Dakini, come under my power
　　　Let me not
　　　slip a shade below
as your eyes see more of me than i
remember, evoke what i have been saving,
　　　turn me on
internally　thru awareness
　　　of your redeeming luminosity."

Dead Cat Head

to Steve

in the ambiguity   of the moment
    caught for a spell between two paths,
how can it be considered kindness to have one's
                    tongue cut out?

to be alone and looking
not working, pursuing pleasure, traveling to return
to a waterless shack not on a road to anywhere.
not to trap myself i renounce all i am or have been
all i seem to do and say again and again,
        i renounce   "i renounce"
count in my shy favor; i can hold my tongue

(2)

not only did i choose this life, i was left with it.
this place, the friends i can walk to   are home
at the end of a ceaseless wandering.   there is not another
place or pace but there will be shortly.

on one to turn to to have one's ego manipulated, one is
allowed
the extremes of insecurity, lacking such fundamental
reassurance
            in the recognition of the ungraspable.

(3)

to be trapped, caught, tamed and taught to fear
beyond the safety of the cage.
                    to be set free.

First Supai Poem

today i found a square nail
        in indian cliff ruins
lost a colt on distant rim

the sound of wind thru canyon
        cottonwoods   all the branches
                move different ways
the flapping lightly of dry clothes
the rare sound of john montoya
blowing out or grunting in semi-sleep
one room wood house
oil drum stove, two beds
this table
wood washed smooth with use.

"hey billll
what did you dooo?
with my horse?"

Indian Granary Circle

in the middle of the circle
dancing around you
hundred of years ago

on a ledge
wide enough to feel safe on
back from
       the edge
drop off   sharp
hundreds of feet
to canyon below

    from circle's center
you can see the door
in the side of cliff
   on the opposite wall
there   this morning
i look back
    the other way
however you
  look at me.

Old Ways

Everything at hand if the hand be skilled—
rock chipped to edge, fibers twisted and wove.
Not a bite of meat retained by the hunter
but all given freely,
and as freely all favors returned.
Not an animal or bird brought down but its spirit
asked permission, its flesh regarded as a gift.
Not a season without a song
from back when they spoke like us.
Not a moment when all one big family
was forgotten by being stingy.
But a life woven like a basket
starting where it ends,
    wound so tight by care
    it holds water.

"The Delighted Dancer Filled With Rapture"

"Under the Moon Over Undomesticated Lands",
    "Don't Fall in Love With Me," I sang

      as i reached my grasp fell
      what i chased i chased away
         nothing to cling to
      my honesty unleashed
        a sad farewell.

      i soon realized
      if i withdrew, my touch
        would return.   your interest
      could be worn out by persistence
      but awoke
        when no attempt had been made.

Fertility level

drain well
give back what you take
don't work when it's wet
or make produce more than it's nature

work deep
mix up the levels

legumes
vetch
hold it together
help it drain

clean renegade seeds off machinery
tools, socks, pants cuffs

you reap what weeds
you let take hold.

Melon

(to John Staple)

Old man Crenshaw lived in Durham
   "orange fleshed, yellow fleshed,
white fleshed,   web skin, sugar skin
  ripe around here bout august."

lets em get soft 'n juicy
  so's can be smelled 6 feet off.

"In the early morning" crazy earl sez
  "a ripe watermelon -cracks-
       at the sound of your feet."

Wild Song

element of fear
    of animals as one walks thru dense brush
as much to warn away as
        command one's own emotions.
must be in terrified apprehension
    of being disrespectful
of the dead who leave traces
as you step upon wide stone
or pick up a chipped rock.
must get the singer lost, steal
    the singing breath away.

resonance surrounding held notes
    is the clue that something
beyond mere personal
        is sounding thru
    speaking to
comfort you.

Petroglyphs

the wind from the valley blows harder
louder over the petroglyphs
on a granite outcrop
high over the upper Yuba valley.
across the space up to the east;
      old man mountain.
to south on the other side
interstate 80, highway 29
   and the railroad.

maybe
perfection of painting body
for protection
so could paint stone,
ancient by time indians arrived.
"they were there before we came."

when we're replaced
as we,
those native living here,
petroglpyhs
will scarcely be more ancient.

   Animals will still know
guardians long permeated
by the symbols on stone,
the hypnotized
   inspired
messengers
   from before.

before words, understanding

before words, understanding.
before division, sharing and giving forth
before leaving, will waited feeling left behind-
  wife light waning, clan just gone, a guardian
    driver of drivers, friend of those driven,
smiling at her careful not to show he knew.

edge of grand canyon   now returning
remembering "sister" lastnite lover still kindly
    held firm in my brother's arms
  on the rim   the void we face together
   him with woman, playing strings,
    eating and smoking, holding and stroking
hair   skin   eyes   clothes she   her

We are beyond ourselves, we mean more than can
be made or done, see beyond sight, know beyond
any words to express, give what can
never be taken, open and even vulnerable, easily
woundable but without fear, waiting
       with certainty and patience.

O—
  I stood under moon light at rim top
  bathed in breaking bliss.

Wisdom Road

(if sung, repeat first 3 verses)

been a long time
since i walk down wisdom road
but i still remember
how it feels to glow.

when you eat wisdom
tastes bitter on the tongue
but now's time to know for sure
while we're still bold and young.

got to open your mouth
let the song come out
got to close your eyes
to know what will later be
got to open them to really see
but no one can walk down
      wisdom road for me.

don't make me use my poisons
i've kept them down so long
if you make me win a battle
you've made me wrong.

you got to pretend you're glowing
even when she doesn't make you glow
remember what you've got to offer
be thankful, when it's time to go.

So-called Spirit Helpers

"let's get drinking & sing songs!" they
say "smoke a pipe and listen
for those deep within feelings"
"what happened to open old potlatches?
-give a big time, see everybody have fun."

    but when you need a helper
how much help are they then?

              ✍

Coyote

You're the same as Coyote
when you forget who you are

that's all he ever did!

Nov 17 Sutra

nanao speaking to lowell & me

in desert cave, so light, so strong. far
from moving graveyard—vast ghost town
visited by millions of weekend tourists
                one last time.

Had i the chance; priests
for calm end of survival; faint
when realizing how far is left to walk.

motionless in trance, open-eyed coma,
        no consciousness.   my spirit listening,
leaves me   vacant   to soar   so far—

goodbye people civilization roles actors,
goodbye future goodbye life, there is no life.
only;   Bright silence of the sun.

        Fasting;
completely stop outside...try by yourself,
from inside; then you see whole world
(not small part the "agents" display
"we are content cause it doesn't seem worthwhile
to get ahead of anybody"
so suffer the same   limitations as they.)

to cut off all desire; that is biggest desire
        ("possible to disenchant yourself
            by indulgence to grow more tired?")

need so strong inner demand
        you can't have desire.
                cleaning,
cleansing power, desire comes up at first
but such a power   changing to cleansing power—
you become desire itself

then you forget desire, you are nothing.
no life, no future, no like or dislike,
no individuality;
if you have desire
                    you have individuality
but if you have no more desire
                    you are no more individual.

God is silence, keeps always silence
mt. stream bubbling—carrying down to ocean,
emptiness and eternity same ocean,
emptying to emptiness, giving more—easily,
                learning to give more easy.

I went to see the sage

suspected of escaping
he wanted to throw me back
    on the wheel.
but i'm no dharma heir
transmission specialist,
dragon mien glorious
bearing the fragrance
    of flowers from afar.

꩜

Omen Bearer

i went to the sunken pond
sat on its steep crumbling gravelly slope
spied a bucket floating
in clay colored water.
i sat and felt all thru me
gave in to every physical influence
my body yielding as my mind of nerves
withdrew into me peacefully
then looked at that bucket
sang "turn around...turn around..."
and the bucket
gently at first
turned around.

The Deer

The ineluctable fatality of destiny
wounded, the coyotes appear, and the chase commences.
Little by little   the chased is noted to tire
            -the coyotes close in.

To the most beautiful in the fullness of life
there appear the obscure messengers of destiny
and beauty, power, grace   are not enough.

El Venado

La ineluctable fatalidad del destino;
herido, aparecen los coyotes, y la caza comienza.
Poco a poco el perseguido se nota fatigado
            -los coyotes alcanzan.

En lo mas feliz de la plenitud de la vida
aparecen mansajeros oscuros del destino
y la belleza, el poder, la gracia   no bastan.

Red Rock Road

(to the builder of the Bear Dance Sweat House)

Fire iron/golden center/pumice
pottery vessels, glazes.
   sun thru roof
  spirits smell and come down
clarity of desert hot springs
old longings vanish in heat
    rarified
   "just follow the red road."

2

nice looking black haired half breed woman
holding the bones, wanted to
play with her all night
  where is she?
hair down to thighs
  "don't know how long it
   was down there"
Tom points to crotch.
Vessel, glaze center

to get luck with women
"all you need's a hard on."

Excerpts from Bristlecone Pine

sagebrush pale green
wind skinned legs on bare shale
ground strewn with power sticks
we feel no need to touch.

trees emerge around each bend on north slopes.
being not so numerous
each can be all the more prized.

cones on green branches spring
from seemingly lifeless trunks
worn smooth with sharp edges
by sand sleet rain and snow
            relentless.

***

a smooth tongue shows a skilled liar,
but a good way to bluff;
pretend you're thinking it just then;
    " i can see it now
        as if before my very eyes"
hand motions and smiling gestures
        can fill the hesitations.

The many slender trunks of bristlecone tremble.
small needled clusters sway on barked branches,
sharp knives and demon forks flash   into
High Altitude, which is also behind   and below us.

***

under the edge of tree cut sky, to them
the song must be tasted like a wind;
time has washed clean all frailty;
only the true survives, the essential core,
all else...   washed clean, blown away.

bare bristlecone
points the way
the earth ascends through space

silence of so long, underneath instinctual
silence of so long, underneath, intuitive
it is the earth our body cuts
the sun lit sky with, in the shadow
in the shade resting too long
     we don't do anyone any good
        we're not in jail.

hilltop, different from a canyon
bristlecone, different from cottonwood
connected without trail
grafted to the same memory
visionary run, where you can have all
you've ever wanted the way you always
wanted it, as much as you rapture-filled
want, delight in, desire, or
you can take the path that no one has ever trod
or ever will again, alone or with the diminishing band,
sing the oldest songs, those never sung
or cease being sung, somewhere deep
within the heart of this oldest tree,

         ***

as the sun set chilly
thru four needle clusters
    we stand over looking down
on sierra snow shadow'd range
     go for the car
     while light remains.

Dissolute But Not Extinct

I throw a piece of carrion
to two wild beasts
to see them fight and claw each other.

To burn myself foolishly
I carried
a torch against the wind.

I was bequeathed a chest of gold
but all these years I kept it closed.

I, a dog, gnaw on a dry bone
        smeared with blood
until utterly tired and frustrated.

I, the mother's breast the child avoids
        of its own volition,
because I am bitterly anointed.

anointed, smeared, thrown
burned and kept closed.
Avoided, gnawed, and bequeathed -
I'd have it no other way.

Poem of a CPITS Poet Working

(1)
I like the sound of silent
    intent concentration
punctuated by rapid pencil strokes
    in white hot inspiration

a class full of them
so the tapping of thoughts
sounds like hard rain
printing wetness
on a distant window.

Second Part of Dr. Montoya's Sermon

(Specialist in Perspiration Purgatives and Melodic Tonics)

"THE LAW mean:
somebody get in trouble.

"If I grab and kiss another
man's wife and someone reports me
to that lady judge
and I get in trouble
that's the law.

"I'm pretty smart
but I'm no good."

Already Wet

English Version of the song by Montoya, in Supai

went to the dance
with woman so innocent and sweet
i turn my head
she slip outside
  just 2 or 3 minutes
when she slide inside
i feel her slippery thighs
  Already Wet
  Already Wet
she was a sweet one, sure
but she go outside a few minutes
 come back in slippery
  Already Wet
  Already Wet

Stuck craw

last night dreamed very pretty
musical voiced woman.
last time i dreamed this
John told me, "too bad, that angel
maybe going up to heaven
if not get right.
Better to dream living old woman
or open young child
then you can have more power with womans
when you talk to them, can talk
to child or animal, anything..."
that was the time he told me
"We are going to take you
to Montoya Mountain
and murder you right there.
Then come back
and take your wife to town.
We'll all have fun together
          except you."

Rooster Song

for dead man

Before the good rooster holler
...early in the morning, dark
get up early
I'm a rooster too!
get an early start-
  an hour later;
  not so early,
    too bad.
    ...but before the rooster
  before the good rooster
    holler!
early in the morning.

Hit 'em in the hind quarter
we go in a hurry to hill top
    15 miles
you don't know how to follow the trail
Your first time?
  Get an early start
saddle your horse in the dark
so you can when you dead
for that last ride up
early in the morning dark
before the rooster
before the good rooster
    holler.

Died on the Trail

I talk to him at his grave
   am led to where the red clay buried lay.
It seems you'll never understand me
     caught in the traps of this world
   I just hope you're happy in what you do.
I went with some crazy boys.
I went with some crazy boys.
   The packer thought him drunk, kept on going
   he was still wearing my hat when he was found.
Earlier some riders saw him
singing songs under an overhang.
After they had each eaten two datura Webb said
   Go ahead, I'll stay here
   there's nothing back down there calling me
   nothing down there for me
   we'll meet again somewhere else
   in another place.
Maybe he was feeling good so took more.
   He had no water, no one gave him any
   or knew to make him throw up.
   The August Sun sucked his water.
The August Sun face up
   burned out the last of his life.
     ...You'll never understand me
     caught in the traps of this world...

Montoya Powwow

for Webb Jones

"sing three, four times   everybody cry
feel sorry one or three minutes is enough
sing for the dead man.

"that mean business   no telling lie
no coming back to see you friend

"sing all night   no burying
just 'burn 'em UP' before dawn
no more come back to see you
burn up   no bury
having a powwow all night
in the morning   using kerosene
strike matches   burn 'em up
fire going down
no more come back   the end.

"not like bible
or white people telling
dead man gone   he can't come back
goodbye Gone Went   NO MORE
he can't come back
burn 'em up..."

To Fall To

the leaf
    has all
the time
      in the world
  to fall to

earth

III.

Right Straight Through

Recognizing Looks

very polite
east oakland party
    "choose your vice" a sly friend said
Shady women weave around the room
    as if on missions the lights go out
the music is so loud everyone's submissive
some people high, you don't know what's
    coming on from the punch
people recognize you haven't seen for years
    jr. high school pachucos
        and also in the crowd
one or two other doctors, recognizing looks,
one or two old friends fade into the dark
with girls and do not
        ride back home.

Invite

wind around the shack
blows fierce
    willows and phone wires
sway violent
sage brush piles up
on deserted car bodies
is swept away

wind loud thru the walls
sand hits windows
    comes in thru door cracks
rugs blow off tree limbs
a whirl is trapped in stove pipe.

connoisseurs of thirst could converse
in appropriate rite,   o desert rat

if a calm arises
obsidian chips litter foothills

but do not wait, old friend
until the mountains
        lose their snow.

"Remember the Poor - It Costs Nothing"

–josh billings

it's easier to be poor
than to worry about money.
 when money comes in
 things have a price   instead of a value.

i'm not putting you down
i just can't live up to your style.

        aging and impoverished
on the fringes of literary society
        am i depressed?   no.
I'M CLAUSTROPHOBIC
        without a scapegoat
        or a self justification
i don't even have the distraction
        of spending money.
...of course when i have a full-time job
i won't have time to think like this
                or write it down.

Skunky

I wish I could cage her
  who tries to enter my bed
who cleverly reaches in and grabs my cheese
spills my silver, opens my door
pulls clothes off hangers, craps on the floor.
I am learning love.
        Love what I can't control.
Unwilling I feed, provide
              an exciting place to stay.
She's not afraid, pokes her head out in daylight
with sparkling eyes. I go and stick
my nose and eyes a foot from her
              and blow in her face

      She's company...
            but not good company.

Him

The guy
my ex had a crush on
walks into the bar
a year and a half after
      she left.

I once knew how
to spell his initials
      with bullet holes
now I've forgotten his name.

Right Straight Thru

All thru grade school
other kids
made arrows go thru hearts

i never understood why

twenty-five years later
writing a valentine
to my ex-wife

I understand

The More I Stare

The more I stare
at waterfall
the more emotions fall
    off my face
the more
    "what's me"
is washed away
so the one behind
    my face is left
like the face of rock
    water
         falls
     over.

3 Sisters

it's all only
energy, she claims
feeling good or bad
is completely one's choice.

another advises
the only way to escape one's fate
is to enjoy it.

the last convinces me
we are our own reward.
her irony and delight
were not lost.

Waits

My body, late at night, waits
my mind knows
         you'll never come
but my body--

The Woman of Dawu

I

The widest, brightest smile
   shines from her broad Tibetan face
      with brilliant eyes
she stares at me nearly two hours
smiling all the while
as I stare and smile at her
and the dust and the streets
and the Han and the horses
and the children   crowding
in their blue or green Chinese caps
dissolve
and only us in all the world
on that street of Dawu

II

And the woman of Dawu has great wealth
of silver and turquoise down her back
and her hair in one hundred eight braids
and her body   has the grace
and the strength of an animal of the wild
and of a woman who can tame
and she walks, not proud
but as if
the universe were hers
and it is.

III

The woman of Dawu has a child;
with dusty matted black hair
and bare dirty feet
and a single cotton garment.
She holds and talks to that child
and gives her suck
as the Han girls point
at her lovely breast.

That child is of all the children of the world
the wealthiest
as the arms
and the words
and the laughter
and the smile of the woman of Dawu
are hers.

IV
And when I say I can spend my life
beneath the yak blanket of the woman of Dawu
and never have cause for regret,
call me a fool: say
I have no way of testing my assumption.
You do not see her smile
nor will her smile for me ever stop
          forever.

V
And at forty below, dung steams
   under the edge of the tent
   smoke turns my skin dark
   wind flaps prayer flags in frenzy.
         In the morning
she lights juniper
and evil is kept away
her prayers slip between us as mani beads
and her prayers are answered.
   She lies beside me happy
   and falls asleep full of warmth
and wakes beside me happy
   then gently turns
and looks into my face.

Some Other

in some other world
we still rub in sleep
   sending off sparks.

Someone else's touch

when a man lives the lie he has to live
to lie with the woman he loves
is he still worthy of that woman's love?

when his touch does not excite
as much as she thinks   someone else's touch
would excite   should he touch her?

should he let on
        that the thrill is getting gone
or should he simply savor
        that sad sweet bit of pleasure
pretending nothing much feels wrong?

There Are Tests

there are tests, she said
what kind? I asked

when you change
who you really are
to please me

you fail.

Venus in Scorpio

I knew when we first met
you were going to break my heart
but since it wasn't going to happen right away
I thought, "so what?"

Without enough
of a heart to break
I thought I could stand it.

By the time

by the time
a woman gets me
to that point
where she can have all of me

I'm no longer worth having.

Afraid of Showing

I've been so careful
    not to show my hurt
        I didn't notice it myself.

This attentive alert
    mask of my wound
        I'm afraid of showing.

Lest it humiliate me further
    lest I be seen as needy
        and so be avoided.

I never recovered
    tho she immediately
        got on with her life.

I've been a loser
    these last 10 years
        where once I was a winner.

Both have their stresses
    both are utterly empty.

The loser life
    is just as good as that of a winner.

    you never have to live up
        to your previous peak

    and you could at anytime
        stage a remarkable comeback.

I Hate the Men You Sleep With

I hate the men you sleep with
        "hit 'em on the head
        push 'em off a cliff
        kick 'em behind

        makes no difference"

each one more slippery
than the one before.

Tho unaroused when you came out
        to me in the night
to lay your head on my shoulder
        I should have taken you away
rather than see you soon walk past
        with one I thought beneath you,

        but what do I know?

Small Doses

she got so good
at keeping me guessing
I stopped guessing.

❦

Thank You

Thank you friend
who kicked me
when I was down.

You inspired me
to rise up on my own feet
a posture
I might not otherwise have
considered.

If

if indeed my ego was destroyed
when you left me for who you did
              for who you're with now
        for just about anyone as long
                    as he's not me
if my ego was destroyed because you got bored
with my love, bored with making love to me
      are delighted with others
if my ego was destroyed because nothing
      we ever had turns you on
          while others turn you on
then let my ego be destroyed.

When Coyote

when coyote
is dropped out of an airplane
on a moonless winter night
does he land on his feet?

no.

on his heart.

Supervisor

Something in how you regard me
        mystifies
as if you had some secret
    inner knowledge
    behind your observation
but i have been fooled
    into doubting myself
        by wiser men than you.

When you lose control
    'you have lost control'

        speak to me in a whisper
yell at someone else.

꘏

16 Days

it wasn't the degradation of submission
or the demeaning labor
i like that part for religious reasons.
  nor the fact that i couldn't
  talk down to a dog;
nor the sign:
"no insubordination will be tolerated"
when insubordination is my best asset.
it wasn't the threat
    that the shareholders could sue me
    if a mistake were made
nor the tone of voice
    that startled me
having gotten up so early to be there
    for so little...
or the long drive that exhausted me

        no,
    it was when i found my tee shirt
that i had sweat wet
hung to dry on my truck for the trip home
on the earth
    run over tire-treaded
that was it!
    i'd be a coward not to quit!

"Dear Ben"

(Mechanic at Meadowmont Chevron)

Whether your gross negligence
strays over into the criminal
only a court would know.

Your lack of responsibility or concern
may be a public danger
the community should be warned of.

Not only for my sake
whose car you set on fire
but to protect others
you should be forced to pay
much more than money.

But your time's not
worth much either.

Sierra Love Note

empty high sierra cabin
one room, table, bench
   a note on a nail
by the one window
   "the day you're due
   I rise before dawn
if I know you'll be here at 4
I'm already happy at noon"

 -you love not when you wish
   but when you love-
when you're older it's no different
   it just takes longer.

intricate swift   free
   no grasp   or clutch

  held invisibly, save
the barest passing touch.

IV.

Recognizing Grin

How the Mattole River Rd. Got Open

Dick stopped the King Cab
and asked if I was all right
as I struggled up the hill
   to Freeman's house
tossing rocks off what was left of the road.

Once I was squeezed inside with Joe,
they asked if I'd continue up the hill
with them to check on Joe's cabin
   and house, move rock and branches
off the road, help rescue
     anyone caught under a
      flattened house.

Coming down the hill
Dick offered a proposition
He wanted to open the road to let the folks
   trapped on the beach get out while they could.
"I've got a bad heart but a D9
   Joe has a small saw but he's
     not young either
We need someone like you to do
   the hard part, climb around
unsteady ground and choke chain."

I told them
I was the one they was looking for
I'd give them the best I had
   as long into the night
     as I lasted.

Dick (deadpanned) "That's
the first time in a long while
since anyone's made me
An Offer Like That."

෴

None of my consideration

"none of my consideration"
what she's doing   far away
   with someone else.
whenever you go   you leave behind
can't expect it   be as you left.
to be detached   to have a key
that locks the hurt   is not to feel
all there is to feel
but to dwell there   is an indulgence
a cliff climber   can not afford.

John Montoya's Final Benediction

Four first-class doctors
examine
a specimen of blood
ask me about you
all the time.
I told them, the doctors, four of them
you go to all over the place.
I tell them you got nothing
no gonorrhea, nothing.

You go out someplace
way out and stay there four or five days.
Dry up your fingers, your bodies
walk outside.
I'm right,
I'm not wrong.

The doctors check out persons
the lieutenant asked about you.
I tell him you watch me like a doctor
you're my protection, you watch me.
I'm right
I'm not wrong.

By the doctors' orders
the ladies are coming now
to take us to dinner.
Pretty nice lady, big behind
looks beautiful...
going for the dinner
at the dining room
where we eat all the time.

We're going to go
an examination

they're going to watch me pretty close
but I got nothing
everything okay
just forget it.

It's up to you, you're a person
you can go any way you want.

One the indian inspection
   then the white inspection
      different,
   all kinds watch me real close,
I mean to tell
   the big fat woman nurse
   she's supposed to take care of me
or she get fired
   by the white people
   who went down (points) to see
   the old woman.
She doesn't have gonorrhea either
like me.
I got nothing.   That's correct!

The doctors told me to tell you to go
with me to see the first-class nurse.
You're a first-class doctor
   you, the one, my protection
not a regular one
   you a first-class
      the same as the nurse is.

Me too, I can understand very well
wanted to tell you back and forth
   everything's all right.

A person is talking a different way--
If I got mad, well I'm a different
    that's the way it goes--
you can talk a different way
    I can understand
I'm different too, that's correct
    I can understand you
by watching pretty close, like you
    I'm not wrong
        not a regular, no--
           first-class.

It's up to you, you're a person
you can go any way you want.

Ode to a Medicine Man, George Staple, died 11/4/89

You wore a white smock
as you stood counting out pills
with a spatula
behind the counter.
I took the pills in a bottle
with our name on the label
in a bag on my bike
up and down the long streets.
Little old ladies gave me
dimes and quarters.
When I wore a white smock too
they would tell me
how much I looked like you.

No More Hot Coffee When I Die

"No more hot coffee when I die
no more at the sweatbath
no more walk-around."

"all I have to do is a devil
dragging my tail around, looking back
got the horn on, got the ears,
look white, not black."

"sometimes ghosts meet the devil
ghost wear black hat, black coat
black pants, black shoes, black skin
look all dirty and terrible
but the devil not wear anything
just little hair on your leg, all over
then he walk around, nice
but the ghost is pretty bad
under the cave ready to bite
ready to catch you, make you feel scared
under the cave, over there."

"the ghost fighting the devil
but can't do it. The devil try
to hit the ghost but go right through.
they make the cowboy scared
on the trail at night, but the devil
makes you laugh, that's nice
dragging the tail with the horns
give you good luck, the devil."

"no more hot coffee when I die
no more sweatbath
no more walk-around."

Ancient Mastery

in a 6 room pre-fab indian's home
flown from eight miles away
down from south canyon rim:
I wake to moonlight
from a sleep after a hauled in by mule
and bought at the store meal.
only the tortillas and sharing was native
to this land the government
has tried so hard to tame thru
debt credit, dependency and police.
Outside frightened dogs bark back
at long coyote howls, echoing echoes.
magnifying what was and is terror or
ecstatic, WILD -

this thin veneer of white colonial
genocide park service carrying guns
is doomed by an older understanding
that could cope
with the wilderness inside.

ancient mastery, in thee i trust
given the ancient mastery to trust.

Why Crime is Unavoidable

Because our attitude is all important
    when talking to the police
who at any moment for any reason
    can give you a blood test
    break your ribs, put you in jail for life.
Because not to answer any question
    even if it seems of a personal nature
not to obey any order even if scared
(as you're being probed for any sign of resistance
        so they can get you for a real beef
    and have some fun besides
        breaking a few bones
    showing how tough they are
            overwhelming one)

    is illegal
and they can make as much evidence
    as needed to put away
any who come to their notice
    showing a defiant spirit

    ...attitude is all important.

꿈

Self-Fulfilling Prophecy

the more you treat prisoners
as less than fellow humans
the more they become
less than fellow humans

perhaps they will find you
after their release
you who would treat another
as less than a fellow human

lessons of cruelty
are often well learned.

Law-Abiding

People would be more law-abiding and secure
if there were fewer laws they had to obey.
That is the only way to stop the war
which had to destroy this country to save it.

Anger makes you more intelligent,
but intelligence in the wrong company
can get you killed.

When we have humane police
who don't have to carry guns because
there is no reason to enforce
unpopular or invasive laws,

then we will be a free people.

    Vice is not a crime
there is more to freedom
    than the free dumb to conform.

The puritans disagree
the inquisition, secret police
    confiscators, turnkeys
fanatics, zealots, persecutors
prosecutors,
judges, disagree, yet

Vice Is No Crime.

When humane police don't need to carry guns

    we will, as a people,
    be free.

The Only Way To Reduce Crime
is to Make Fewer Acts Illegal

The real criminals
           are not the ones
     behind the bars
but those who put them there:
       (who locked them in?)
who created the
   inequities
and vast disparities
who manipulate,
     force
another into inevitable crime,
who invent crimes
   to generate revenue...
who live in a police state
who deny there is a police state
     until stopped and then asked,
  "Will you please get out of your car?"
who thrive where the environment, the place,
   its spirit is not taken into account, shown by
not cleaning up afterwards,
    only getting all you can
        and getting out quick.

I do not want to know.
Let others hunt down the oppressors as they flee,
I have been angry too many days of my life.
I resolve to stop stalking the path
   of my wound,
to forgive personal inequities I cannot right,
    trusting   in divine retribution
      if there be a vengeful God,
and poetic justice,   notwithstanding.

Hard Being So Good

I hope Wild Bill brings something bad,
    real bad.
It's hard being so good when you can still
    taste it, you can still smell it, want
    just a touch, a taste, a hit that
    hits hard into easy, real bad-
like Bill maintaining bad habits
    nearly all have abandoned for health
    peer pressure, sadomasochist punishments
given by legal representatives of the people's will
against those people they are to serve,
    pain their reality principal, no touch
    their rule, "Genocide is just western
civilization's way of saying hello." says Bill, wildly,
as I eye his shirt pocket for the bulge of a stale
camel or american spirit. "The only crime worse
than giving an order is to obey one," I respond,
    relaxing my outer facial and body tension
    so I don't show I'm jones'n for a smoke.
To appear too eager
in the presence of a shadowy trickster
    who lets his light shine, would be,
well, to appear too eager.

Thief

Poet as thief
　gives everything away
　　both miracle
　　and wondrous crime;
A liar who always tells the truth.

Somehow affairs of state rest
on tired poet shoulders
even while avoiding an Empire
　in a forest cabin.

Somewhere near true wilderness
　sometimes before dawn
sitting upright on my bed in the dark
a whisper from some disincarnate
　predecessor
moves my heart.

Four Stones

While singing to the four stones
    Heal me   Heal me
then itemizing my afflictions
    rage at the cops
        dissatisfaction with my station, career
   my own weakness before state cruelties
     confiscations, war lust, impoverishment
    my fear that keeps me from meeting my need...
    Heal me   Heal me

I prayed with song to stones
A Hawaiian lady my age
    modestly attired with bright red lips
       joined me in my devotions
    placing an orange on a stone
praying in Hawaiian and snatches of English
(make me strong for what lies ahead, I heard)
then placing the same offering on the next stone
     praying again
Our eyes crossed & touched
    her prayer continues as did my song
but we each took what nourishment and pleasure
    from each other as was so remarkably available
maybe a little mutual curing was going on just then
I felt it, and I saw her draw it in
    and give it all away as well.
she continued unhesitantly to the next two stones
    in the ring of four;
Ended her supplication, disappeared
       before I thot to follow.

Come Now

the wealth of empires
flowed thru my fingers

wise ones and seers
gave me precise maps.

after so much searching
    years of hard travel
why is it that i now come to you?

no longer a question
no longer anything to ask for
I come empty
amazed and wonderdumb

why is it that I come now to you?

Zendo Meadow

too few nights
have fallen asleep

staring at stars

Polar Bear Head #1

Rita
was Lowell's girl
in the smallest
    house in Nevada City.

It was so small
she cut off the
    head
so she could put her rug down.

I got the head
and fitted its teeth
    around the front luggage rack bar
    on top of my old VW bug
I drove it like that
    for a year

the eyes staring
straight ahead
down the road.

Poem Requested by Nanao to be Put on a Scarf

I'm never lost
in forest or town

because I never care
    where I am

☙

North from Shelter Cove

Setting my pack down the stony beach
lulled by wave sounds
and the weight I carry
I look up to see an old coot
bearded, wild eyed, with his pack,
        coming toward me from the way I'm going.

With a recognizing grin
out goes his hand before him
        his thumb stuck straight up.

I had never met him before
        tho I've known him all my life

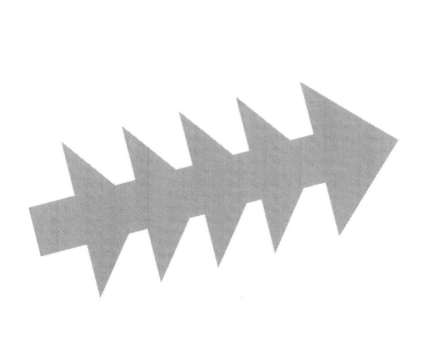

Acknowledgments

The poet wishes to express unending gratitude to the editors of:

Caterpillar; Kyoi; Coyote's Journal; Bits and Snatches; Kuksu; An Alleghany Star Route Anthology; Passes for Human; Coyote Run; Snowy Egret; Deepest Valley Review; New Directions 42; Mind Moon Circle; The Shadows of Light; Morning Thunder Poems; Beloit Poetry Journal; City Lights Review; Gate; Art Matters; Poet News; Gary Snyder, Dimensions of a Life; Beneath a Single Moon; Dr. Montoya's Medicine; I Hate the Men You Sleep With; The Only Way to Reduce Crime is to Make Fewer Acts Illegal; A Coyote Reader; Blind Donkey; Glyphs; Community Endeavor; The Dagger; Tangram Press; California Poets in the Schools Anthologies; Earth First Journal; Something Else; and any others that I may have forgotten.

Special thanks to Steve Nemerow and Fred Brunke for invaluable editorial assistance; to Gary Snyder, Lawrence Ferlinghetti and Phil Whalen for their encouragement; and to Kenneth Rexroth and John Montoya of the Havasupai tribe for their lasting influence.

About the Author

Will Staple lives in a cabin in the California foothills. He grew up in Oakland under the shadow of the Beats, and attended UC Berkeley during the Free Speech Movement. From 1970 to 1995 Will published over 200 poems infused with the Grand Canyon and mountain forests on the sassy, sexy side of spirituality, filled with a sly humor, condensed form, depth of content, detailing the culture that left the cities in the 1970s for a more archaic path with a heart.

Books published in this time period are: *Passes for Human, Coyote Run, I Hate the Men You Sleep With, The Only Way to Reduce Crime Is to Make Fewer Acts Illegal,* and *Dr. Montoya's Medicine.*

Made in the USA
San Bernardino, CA
10 March 2018